JUMBO JACK'S COOKBOOKS

AUDUBON MEDIA CORPORATION
AUDUBON IA 50025 • 1-800-798-2635

HOW TO TALK HOOSIER

By

Netha Bell

Quixote Press
1854 - 345th Avenue
Wever, Iowa 52658

IV

★ ★ ★ ★ ★ ★ ★ ★ ★ ★ ★

ISBN 1-57166-050-X

Quixote Press
1854 - 345th Avenue
Wever, Iowa 52658

PRINTED
IN
U.S.A.

VI

Dedicated To

My beloved son and daughter-in-law,

Jim and Anita Albert

and to

My "baby" brother and sister-in-law

Don and Linda Carter

Acknowledgements

I would like to say "Thanks" to my good friends and neighbors, Doris and Donnie Beelman and Marlene Barnes, for their support, encouragement, and contributions.

And To:

Ethel Richman, librarian at the Cattermole and Idol Rashid libraries.

Preface

When the building of railroads in Indiana shifted the early Hoosiers north from the Ohio River, those folks brought more than their wagons and skillets. They brought their language.

How To Talk Hoosier tells of some of the words and phrases of Indiana today.

Introduction

Netha Bell has captured Hoosier talk in her book *How To Talk Hoosier.*

Some of these words and phrases might not be the King's English, but they are Hoosier to the bone.

Prof. Phil Hey
Briar Cliff College
Sioux City, Iowa

A BIRD BRAIN:

… has nuthin' to do
with those fine
feathered friends.
It is a stupid or
foolish person, as in, "Tessie is
such a bird-brain."

A BLOCKHEAD: Doesn't really have a
head made of wood — just acts that
way.

A CHIMLEY:
… is that brick,
four-sided thing
up on your roof
that Santa Claus
comes down at
Christmastime.

A COWPATH:

… is not like
a bridle path
that you ride
horses on. It's a fenced pathway that leads from
the barn to the cow-pasture.

AGE BEFORE BEAUTY:

… usually said about who goes through a doorway
first. The reply is, "No!! Dust before the broom!"

A GREENHORN:

… is what a farmer calls a city slicker that moves to
the country and tries to make a livin' at farmin'.

A GULLY-WASHER:

… is a hard rain. It might be rainin'
cats and dogs, pitchforks and hammer handles,
or be a fine day for the ducks.

A HOLLER:

… is a small
valley
between
two hills.

A JERKWATER TOWN: is a small town or village where trains didn't have a regular stop, but they could fill up their boilers while still going at full speed by lowering a scoop into a water trough located between the rails.

ALLEY-APPLE: ... is a piece of horse manure, as in, "Doncha step on the alley-apple over there."

ALL-IN: tired or exhausted, as in, "Man, I tell ya, I'm all in from all that gardenin'."

All-OUT: complete, as in, "He made an all-out effort to git that roof fixed 'fore it rained."

ALL-TO-PIECES: out-and-out, excessively, as in, "I beat him at chess all to pieces."

AN INDIAN-GIVER: is not the act of giving a Native American to someone else. It's one who gives a gift and then wants it back.

AN IRISH NIGHTINGALE: doesn't refer to a nurse or bird of Irish descent. It's a bullfrog!

INDIANA SWINGER:

... that's a guy that wears bib-overalls and no underwear.

AS BIG AS WHAT HOGS DREAM OF WHEN THEY'RE TOO FAT TO SNORE:

... said of an
obese lady
that occupies
two seats
on an
airplane.

AS FULL OF TWITTER AS A BIRD ON A PERCH:

... usually said
of a frail
little old
lady that
makes a lot
of gestures
during a
lengthy
conversation.

AS MAD AS A BULL AMONG BUMBLE BEES:

Now, the
stinger is,
what wuz
that bull
doin' there
anyhoo??

AS MISERABLE AS CHICKENS IN A RAIN, HEADS DOWN AND TAILS AT HALF-MAST:

… said of a person feelin' <u>mighty</u> low!!

AS NOISY AS A HOG EATIN' WALNUTS:

… said of a noisy, ill-mannered eater.

AS NOISY AS TWO SKELETONS MAKING LOVE:

… the leg bone's connected to the thigh bone, the thigh bone's connected to the hip bone — and all that jazz!! Now THAT'S noisy!!

A SNOW-JOB:

... isn't shovelin' the sidewalk in the wintertime. It's to overwhelm by a tall tale, as in, "Boy! That salesman shur tried givin' me a snow-job.

AS SCARCE AS HEN'S TEETH:

Take my word for it, that's rare. But if you don't believe me, you might want to chase that old hen around the chicken yard and prove it to yourself.

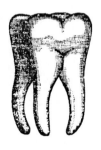

AYR-OH-MA:

That's the odor wafting from a Hoosier kitchen when dinner's cookin'.

BACHLUR GIRL:

… is an unmarried, self-sufficient wummon. She's diffrunt from an old-maid in that an old-maid's nevur bin married — nor nuthin'.

BACK TOCK:

… impudent talk or retort, as in, "Now, son, don't give me none of yer back tock."

BAHR'L

… a barrel, as in, "He shur duz have me ovur a bahr'l!"

BARKIN' UP THE WRONG TREE

… isn't what a no-good dog does whin ya take him a-huntin'.
It's what someone does when they're misinformed.

BARN RAISIN':

… is not the process of starting out with a small building and nurturing it until it becomes a large one. It is the erection of a new barn with the help of neighbors, family, and friends, which is a popular event.

BAR-RER:

… borrow, as in, "He went down to the bank to see iffen he culd bar-rer sum money."

BAWL-BABY:

A Bawl-Baby is someone who's prone to cry, as in, "Oh don't be such a bawl-baby!"

BEAN-POLE:

… has nothing to do with stakin' string-beans. It's a tall, skinny person, as in, "Land Sakes, he ain't nuthin' but a bean-pole."

BEATIN' SOMEONE'S TIME:

… isn't what you do to a clock or watch. It means to go out with another's girl or

boyfriend, as in "Whatcha tryin' to do? Beat my time?"

BEAT THE BAND:

… is to do something excessively, as in,
"Mary was cleanin' the house to beat the band."

BEE:

… has nuthin' to do with the little critter that
makes honey. It's an idea, as in, "She
put a bee in her bonnet."

BEESWAX:

… doesn't have a thing ta do with those little honey-makin' critters that live in hives. It's business, as in, "That's none of your bees-wax!"

BAHR:

That's when a mean old cuss is so tough that he goes out bahr huntin' with a switch.

BIDDY:

… isn't a chicken. It's a prying old woman, as in, "Old Miz Taylor wuz nuthin' but a gossipy old biddy!"

BIGGER THEY ARE, THE HARDER THEY FALL:

... is the fearless defiance of size, as in, "My Ma taught me how to throw a haymaker and said, 'The bigger they are, the harder they fall'."

BIG STINK:

... is not a horrible smell. It's a loud, angry commotion, as in, "Tellin' his boss what he could do with his job shur caused a big stink."

BILE:

... is not the secretion produced by the liver. It is to boil, as in, "Whin

they first got married, she couldn't even bile water without burnin' it."

BLOWIN' HIS KAZOO:

… doesn't mean he's playin' a muzeekel insterment. It means he's braggin', as in," He wuz alla time just blowin' his kazoo."

BLOW ONE'S CORK:

… has nuthin' ta do with openin' a bottle of champagne. It is losin' one's temper, as in, "Ever time I mentioned goin' out with the boys, my wife blew her cork!"

BLOW SMOKE:

… has nuthin' ta do with puffin' on a cigarette. It means to

boast or brag, as in, "All Ted could do was
blow smoke."

BOLLIXED-DUP:

... means to be confused
or mixed up, as in,
"Money matters always
causes me to git
all bollixed up."

BOONDOCKS:

... isn't down by the marina or a harbor. It's some
isolated part of the country, as in, "The Smith
family lived so fur out in the boondocks, that if they
wuz ta start ta town when Miz Smith fust got
pregnant, the baby'd be ready to be born 'fore
they got there." Now, that's a fur piece!

BOONDOGGLE:

To boondoggle is not a breed
of dog. It's to work at a
triflin' task, as in, "My
boss ain't give me much
work lately. Just boondogglin'."

BREAD BASKET:

… it's yur stomach, as in, "Mom-ee!! Johnnie hit me in the bread basket!"

BREEZE IN:

… ain't what the wind does. It means to arrive or enter, as in, "She breezed in 'bout the time the party started."

BUCKET OF BOLTS:

A bucket of bolts is an old dilapidated car that rattles when driven, as in, "Hey, Tom. When ya gonna git rid of that old bucket of bolts?"

BUGABOO:

… is supposed to be a small, evil creature that comes down chimneys and kidnaps naughty children …or so some parents, older brothers and sisters, and babysitters tell kids to to keep them in line.

BULLYRAG:

A bullyrag is not a sweatband worn by an over-bearing person. It is to abuse or scold vehemently, as in, "Quit bullyraggin' me."

BURY THE HATCHET:

No, it's not like playin' cowboys and Indians. It's comin' to an agreement, as in, "Let's bury the hatchet."

BUST A GUT:

To "bust a gut" means
to hurry, as in,
"Nettie busted
a gut to tell
Ed all the latest
office
gossip."

BUTTER UP:

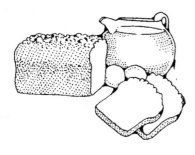

... is not what
you do to a slice
of toast. It means to
flatter someone, as in,
"That sweet young
thing shore did
butter up that rich
old man."

BUTT HEADS:

... is not a new
TV program,
nor does it
have anything
to do with two
billy-goats. It
is when people
oppose each other
in opinions.

CAT GOTCHER TONGUE?:

… can't speak? Asked
of someone not
answering guestions
or contributing to
the conversation.

CATTY-CORNERED:

… diagonal across
from, as in, "The
druckstewer is
catty-cornered
from that
eatin'
joint down the
street."

CHEW THE FAT:

That's when
two old geezers
get together,
sit down and
talk a spell.

CHOW-HOUND:

… is not a breed of dog. It's a hearty-eater, as in, "That kid is growin' lika bad weed, and, boy, is he a chow-hound."

CITY COW:

City cow is bottled or packaged milk.

CLOBBERED:

… hit, as in, "Boy, Jake shur clobbered Pete in that boxin' match."

COAL-OIL:

… kerosene, as in, "Will ya git sum coal-oil fer this lamp whin ya go ta town?"

COOK-KUP:

… has nuthin' ta do with preparing' a meal. It means to make up a story or alibi, as in, "The two men got tagether and tried ta cook-kup a story as ta where they'd bin."

COUNTRY BUMPKIN:

… is what city slickers call someone who lives in the country and doesn't git ta town very often. They also call them a hick or a hayseed.

CRACKLINS:

... are the crisp residue of hog fat after the lard is fried out.

CRADLE SNATCHER:

A cradle snatcher is not someone who kidnaps a baby. It is a person that marries someone much younger.

CRAWFEESH:

... isn't one of them little things in a crick that makes good feesh-bait. It's to renege or back out of sumpthin'.

CRAZY-BONE:

... is not the thick skull of some weirdo. It's the point of yer elbow, as in, "Ow!! I hit my crazy-bone!"

CRY UNCLE:

... doesn't mean yer callin' fer yer aunt's husband. It means ya give up in defeat, as, "I'll let ya up if ya cry uncle."

CUT-SNOW-ICE:

... isn't the precip in the winter time. It means that it has no effect, like, "I don't care what she says. It cut-snow-ice with me."

CUT-UP:

… isn't like mowin' yer yard. It means to joke or play pranks, as in, "He's a regular cut-up."

DAR-TER:

… is the sister to your son, as in, "I hadda give away my dar-ter at her weddin'."

DEAD HORSE:

… isn't an animal they make glue and dog food out of. It's an issue that no longer has any effect on the present, as in, "Now that they've gotten a divorce, whether he cheated on her or not is a dead horse."

DEAD RINGER:

... shur ain't a telephone that's out of service. It's a person that very closely resembles someone else, like, "She's a dead ringer fer my cousin's wife. Dadburned if she ain't!"

DEAD TO THE WORLD:

... means fast asleep, as in, "I tried ta wake my husband when I heard a loud noise downstairs, but he wuz dead to the world."

DEEP-PO:

… depot, as in, "We had ta go down to the deep-po to meet the train from Lafayette.

DIG IN:

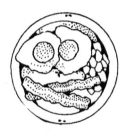

It means to fill your belly, as in, "Fill up yer plate and dig in."

DING-A-LING:

…has nuthin' to do with a bell. It's a screwball or eccentric person, as in, "That gal shur is a ding-a-ling."

DIRT-CHEEP:

It applies to sumpthin'

at an unusually low price, as in, "Boy, he got that tractor at the sale dirt-cheep!!"

DOG-FETCHED:

… is not sumpthin' Rover does with a stick. It's a mild form of swearin', as in, "I'll be dog-fetched if I meant anyone any harm!"

DON'TCHA GITCHER BACK UP:

… means don't git angry, as in, "Don'tcha gitcher back up at what i jist said!"

DOTY:

Doty is the half-rotted wood of a tree or log.

DRAW A BEAD:

It's takin' aim with a gun.

DRECKLY:

… means directly, as in, "Pa, will ya cum help me with this heavy box?" No answer. Then ya repeat it. Still no answer. Then ya yell it.

Now ya hear a voice mumble, "Yah, Ma, I'll be in dreckly."

DROORS:

... underpants, as in, "She had a whole buncha droors hangin' on the clothesline."

DRUCK-STEWER:

...drugstore, like, "Why doncha run down ta the corner druckstewer fer the med'cin?"

DUM AS A DODO:

...to have little gumption, as in, "Even when Harvey wuz a kid, hewuz as dum as a dodo."

EASY AS FALLIN' OFF A LOG:

... means real easy, as in, "Bakin' a dump-cake is as easy as fallin' off a log."

FAMBLY:

... family, as in, "There's shur a lotta kids in the Houston fambly."

FAT AS A COW:

To be fat as a cow means to be really obese, as in, "I seen this here wummin up town 'tuther day that wuz as fat as a cow!"

FEESH:

...what ya catch with a rod and reel outten cricks, ponds, lakes, and rivers. There are catfeesh, carp, crappies (pronounced croppies), blue gill, trout, and bull-heads. After ya git 'em all ketched, ya clean 'em and then ya have a feesh-fry.

FEESH OR CUT BAIT:

... means ta do sumpthin' or let someone else do it, or just plain give up.

FIDDLE AROUND:

To fiddle around means to do sumpthin' half-heartedly or to have an affair, as in, "Jim's wife would kill him iffen she knew he was fiddlin' around."

FLATTERY'LL GITCHA EVERYWHERE — KEEP TALKIN':

... said to somewun who's givin' ya a lot of "soft soap".

FOLLER YER NOSE:

...said to someone askin' directions.

FORENOON:

The forenoon is the morning time before 12 o'clock, as in, "Guess I'd better git ta town this forenoon."

FUR PIECE:

… means "far," or a great distance, as in, "The next town shur was a fur piece down the road." Or it could be a fox scarf or mink stole, as in, "Ma, why dontcha wear that fur piece I gottcha fer Christmas?"

GIT-CHER GOAT:

… to embarrass you, as in, "He wuz jist sayin' that ta git-cher goat."

GIT OFF YER HIGH HORSE:

… has nuthin' ta do with ridin' a tall, four-legged animal. It means quit tryin' ta act so superior.

GIZMO:

A gizmo is a gadget whose name you cain't think of right off hand, as in, "Just take that gizmo layin' on the table over yonder and use it ta crack that nut."

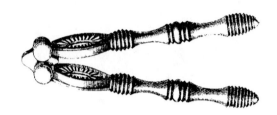

GO CLIMB A SOUR APPLE TREE:

... as in, "When the obnoxious young scalawag asked pretty little Sally Jones fer a date, she jest told him in no uncertain terms ta go climb a sour apple tree."

GOIN' LICKETY-SPLIT:

... is movin' fast.
Or they might be
quick as greased
lightnin', quick
as a wink, going
like a house afire,
hell-bent fer
leather or shakin'
a leg.

GO ON THE WARPATH:

This has nuthin' ta do with
a red-skinned warrior.
It means to get violently
angry, as in,
"When Tom come home drunk the other night,
boy! did his old lady go on the warpath!!"

GOOSE IS COOKED:

... in for trouble,
like, "If yer Ma
sees ya doin'
that, yer goose
is cooked!"

GOTCHA EARS LOWERED?"

... asked of a man who has just gotten a haircut.

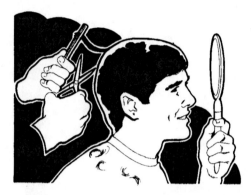

GO TO BAT FUR:
To go to bat fur is to go to someone's aid, as in, "I'd go ta bat fur him anytime."

GOTTA BELLY FULL:

... to have as much as you can take, like, "I set there lis'nun ta that politician and I gotta belly full, so's I jist got up and walked out!"

GOTTA MOUSE INURE POCKET:

... asked of someone that is always sayin' "WE" when they're alone some place.

GREEZY:

... greasy, as in, "Them burgers shur are greezy!" or in, "when oil gits on the hi-way and it rains, ya shur hafta be keerful drivin' or ya slide on that greezy road."

GUFF:

Guff is backtalk,
trouble or
problems, as
in, "Don't
give me none
of yur guff!"

HALF-BAKED:

... is not bread that is dough or half-cooked. It is
something that is silly or unsophisticated, as in
"half-baked idea".

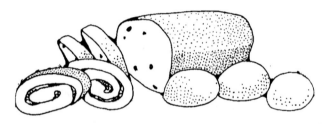

HALF-PAST KISSIN' TIME — TIME TO KISS AGAIN:

... the reply a man might make to a woman who
has just asked him the time.

HANKER-CHEEF:

A hanker-cheef
is whatcha carry
in a pocket or a
purse, or use ta
wipe sweat with.

HAR:

It's what you grow on your head (eeksept fer those
ball-headed guys).

HAVE A HARD ROW TO HOE:

... means gotta difficult task to perform, like,
"That poor old woman shore does have
a hard row to hoe."

HAVE AN AXE TO GRIND:

… is being
angry. Or
they might
be as mad
as an old
wet hen,
mad as a
hornet,

have their dander up, be in a huff, hot under the
collar, peeved, ticked off, or got their Irish up. It
can also mean to have a hidden reason
to do something.

HAVIN' A CONFAB:

Havin' a confab is simply
havin' a conversation,
as in, "We were jist
sittin' 'round, drinkin'
coffee and havin'
a confab."

HAYMAKER:

A haymaker is
a punch ya
lay on somewun,
guaranteed to deck even
the biggest of men.

HE DOESN'T NEED IT ANY MORE THAN A TOAD DOES A POCKET:

… said of someone
who wants
somethin' totally
unnecessary.

HEN-HUZZY:

… a derogatory name for a gossipy woman, as in,
"That old hen-huzzy kepped stickin' her nose
in my business!"

HE PRICKS UP HIS EARS LIKE A FILLY AT FLY-TIME:

... means that he listens intently to what you are saying.

HE SHOOK LIKE A SHIRT IN A HURRICANE:

... said of a coward when he's really scared!

HE SHOULD BE HORSE-WHIPPED:

This has nothin' ta do with being spanked by a member of the equine family. It means that he should be punished severely, like they used to do in the old days here in Indiana.

HE SHOULD BE KICKED TO DEATH BY LAME GRASSHOPPERS:

... this is a mild wish you make against someone that you don't want hurt too badly.

HIT THE CEILING:

This means to become
greatly excited or
angry, as in, "When
I tole my wife
she wuz gittin'
fat, boy! did
she hit the
ceiling!!"

HOB-KNOB

... to associate with, as in, "After the Wilsons won
the lottery, they din't hob-knob with us po' fokes
anymore."

HOG WILD:

When some
of them
dudes from
Indiana
party, they
jist 'bout
go hog wild.

HOLD A CANDLE:

… is not what ya
do down a dark
hallway at
night. It
means to
compare,
as in,
"As far
as singin'
goes, she
cain't hold a candle ta her sister."

HONEST INJUN:

"Honest Injun" does
not refer to an
honest Native
American. It means
"on my honor", as
in, "I'll come over
and help ya with
yer yardwork,
Honest Injun."

HOPPIN' MAD:

... is not what bunny rabbits do when they're angry. It's when people are exceedingly angry or are in a violent rage!

HOS-SKULL:

... is high school, as in, "Our Betsy wuz the fust kid in the fambly ta gradjeate from hos-skull."

IF I HIT YOU, IT'S THE GRAVEYARD —
IF I MISS, IT'S PNEUMONIA:

… is a threat made by a braggart as to how tough he is with a swing.

IF SOMEONE DIES:

… it might be said they cash in their chips, bought the farm, kicked the bucket, are pushin' up daisies, dead as a hammer, dead as a doornail or turned up their toes.

IF SOMEONE IS DRUNK:

… they might be referred to as glassy-eyed, pickled, soused to the gills, cock-eyed; liquored up, stinkin' drunk, tanglefooted, pie-eyed, loaded, tanked-up, plastered, have a snoot-full, crocked, bombed, feeling no pain, sloshed, zonked, blind, in his cups, snockered, three sheets to the wind or half-shot.

IF YOU BET YOUR BOOTS:

... you're saying "yes".
Or you might say you
bet your sweet life,
bet your bottom dollar,
uh-huh, that's
a fact, yes sir-ree,
Bob!, as sure as shootin', I should say so, sure, yup, all rightee, you and me both, you said it, you said a mouthful, absolutely, you're

damn tootin', and how!., you tell 'em, yeah
kee-rect! yowzer, you can say that again, or
right on.

IF YOU SAY "NOT BY A DAMNED SIGHT":

... you're telling
someone "No".
Or you might
say uh-uh, I'm
afraid not, I'm
sorry but, nope,
are you kiddin'?
not on your tin-
type, nothin', doin', no can do, no soap, no dice,
no sale, nah, I should say not!, no way, never,
impossible, or I won't.

I HAVEN'T LAUGHED SO MUCH SINCE MY SISTER KATE CAUGHT HER HAIR IN THE WRINGER:

.... a derogatory remark, usually made by a younger
brother about his older sister.

I LIKE WORK; I COULD WATCH IT ALL DAY:

... usually said by a person as lazy as those loafers on Hee-Haw.

IN A PIG'S EYE!:

... is an exclamation used when you think somethin' is a bunch of nonsense. Or you might say bunk!, fiddlesticks, pshaw, horsefeathers, poppycock, hogwash, applesauce, bull, baloney, that's a bunch of malarky, or that someone is full of prunes.

INNARDS:

Innards have nuthin' ta do with a Swedish chain of motels. It's the insides of a person or animal, as in, "Pa throw them chikken innards out ta the hogs."

IN-NE-MEE:

... is your enemy or foe, as in. "Ya fightcher in-ne-mee durin' a war."

IN OVER HIS HEAD:

... more than he could handle, as in, "When he bought that eeks-spensive new car, and the payments cum due, he decided he'd got in over his head."

IN THE CARDS:

"In the cards" doesn't mean havin' a good poker hand. It means that it's sumpthin' expected, as in, "It was in the cards that they'd gitta divorce."

IN THE DARK:

… means uninformed, as in, "She keeps him in the dark 'bout where she spends all the money."

IN YOUR NECK OF THE WOODS:

… doesn't necessarily mean you live out in the country. It just refers to the area in which you live.

IS YOUR RHUBARB UP?:

… asked of a women if she feels like making love.

IT'S STILL BOLOGNEY; NO MATTER HOW THIN YA SLICE IT:

… it's still a bunch of nonsense, no matter how much you try to prove the opposite.

KEEP YER TRAP SHUT:

… means to shut your
mouth, as in, "Keep
your trap shut,
you hen-huzzy."

KEEP YER EYES PEELED:

… means to be on the
alert and watch what
is going on.

KEEP YER
SHIRT ON:

… doesn't
mean to
stay
dressed.
It means
to just listen
and don't
lose your
temper.

KNEE-HIGH:

When someone is short, they might be knee-high to a: mosquito, grass- hopper, chaw of tobacker, or a tall Indian.

LIE LIKE-A-RUG:

"To lie like-a-rug" means tell fibs or lies, as in, "I ne'er seen no one could lie like-a-rug like that Smith kid."

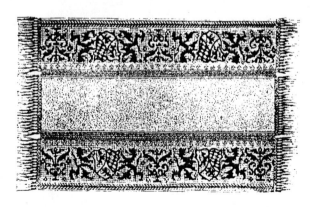

LIGHTNIN' BUG:

... isn't seen durin'
a thunderstorm.
It's commonly
called a firefly
or glow worm in
other parts of
Indiana. "Me
and mah
brother used ta
ketch them
lightnin' bugs
and put them in
a fruit jar ta
make a lantern."

LIKE A COW IN CLOVER:

... when someone is very happy about
something.

LIKE AS TWO
PEAS IN A POD:

... almost identical,
as in "Harry and Sam are as like as
two peas in a pod."

LIKE A SILLY GOOSE:

... when someone is acting like they don't have much sense.

LIKE A KID JUST LET OUT OF SCHOOL:

...when you have no feeling of responsibility and feel a sense of freedom.

LIVIN' IN A GOLD FISH BOWL:

...doesn't mean you swim around and

eat all that flaky food. It means that everything ya do is under close scrutiny by the public.

MANURE SPREADER:

A manure spreader is a machine used to spread fertilizer uniformly. It is the one machine that an implement dealer won't stand behind.

MEAN ENOUGH TO STEAL ACORNS FROM A BLIND HOG:

Now, that's really bein' mean, low-down, sneakin', playin' dirty and being under-handed, don't ya know?

MEAN ENOUGH TO STEAL THE COPPERS FROM A DEAD MAN'S EYES:

This goes back to when the funeral directors put copper pennies on the corpse's eyelids to hold them down.

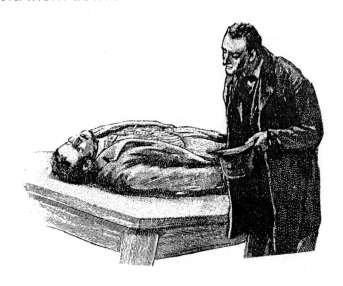

MED-CIN:

Med-cin is what you take when you're sick, as in, "Cum on, Charlie, take yur med-cin like a good boy. It'll make ya feel better."

MILD CURSES:

are phooey, gosh, golly, confound,
doggone, tarnation, thunderation,
criminy, gosh-a-mighty, gosh awful.
gosh all fishhooks, I swan, infernal,
hell-bent, Hell's bells, Ye
Gods!, what the blazes, carnsarned,
by cracky, I'll be jiggered, by
gravy. Lordy, by gum, what the
Sam Hill?, I'll be dogged, dog my
cats, dad-burned, dad-blasted, dad-
rat, dad-gum, Lawdy, shucks, gee
whiz, gee whillikens, by heck,
Holly Mackerel,
Holy Moses, I
don't give a
hoot, for
Pete's sake,
for the love of Mike!, for
cryin' out
loud, Judas
Priest, or
hot diggity!!

MORNER:

... is not someone who weeps at a funeral.
It's like a nooner — only sooner!

MOSEY:

... is not a nickname for the fellar of Biblical fame. It's to move slowly, as in, "Ya'd hafta lighta fire under his tail 'fore he'd quit just moseyin' along."

MULEY COW:

... is not a cross-breed between a cow and a mule. It's either a hornless cow or one that is stubborn. As

in "Old Muley cow come down da track — doo-dah, doo-dah ..."

MUTTON HEAD:

A mutton head is a stupid person, as in, "ya mutton head! Why doncha watch whur yer goin'?"

NEST EGG:

... is the money that is put aside to do ya when the goin' gets tough.

NOT ENOUGH ROOM TO SWING A CAT:

... is a confined area sometimes no larger than a closet. This room is also described as not big enough to change your mind in.

NOTTA WHIT:

… means none, as in, "Ma tuck her tuna cass'role to the picnic and notta whit was left."

OUTTA KILTER:

… means not working right, as in, "The car jist ain't runnin' right. I guess it's all outta kilter."

PEE-KID:

If you are pee-kid, you are looking sickly, as in, "You poor child. Ya shur do look pee-kid this mornin'."

POKE:

A poke is a brown
paper container
in which groceries
are put. Also
known as a sack
or bag.

RED UP:

... to clean up
or straighten
up an area as
in, "While
I'm working
in the kitchen,
you'd better
git in there
and red up
yer room."

SAN QUENTIN QUAIL:

The dictionary says fer quail: that it's a
migratory bird resembling a domestic fowl; or
to draw backin fear; lose courage or cower.
This ain't none of those things ———— I'll
guar-an-tee!! It's an attractive

underaged gal — in other words,
JAIL BAIT!!

SICK AS A DOG:

... to be very ill,
as in, "There
must have bin
sumpthin' in
that salad
that I et that
made me sick as a dog."

SPRING CHICKEN:

... a young,
good-lookin'
person, as in,
"She ain't no
spring chicken,
that's fer shur!"

THAT'S A LONG-TAILED BEAR':

This is what a Hoosier will
say to a person he
is accusing of
lying.

THERE'S MANY A GOOD TUNE PLAYED ON AN OLD FIDDLE:

... said of an elderly
man you thought
was way past the
prime of life — but
apparently isn't!!

THRASHIN' AROUND LIKE A SHORT-TAILED BULL IN FLY-TIME:

... said of someone that
makes excessive
movements of their
posterior region.

TO BEAT ALL HOLLOW:

... to beat thoroughly
as in "I wun that
game of cards to
beat all hollow."

TO BE HUNKY-DORY:

... doesn't mean
that you're one
of those muscle-
bound models in
Playgirl magazine
or in the movies.
It means that every-
thing is fine or okay.

TO BROADCAST:

To broadcast is the
spreading of seeds
in a uniform
manner.

TO COME OUT AT THE LITTLE END OF THE HORN:

That is said of a person that has made big effort in doin' somethin', and then failed.

TO CUT DIDOS:

… is to be frolic-some as in "The little boy was so full of energy that he was cuttin' didos."

TO CUT IT TOO FAT:

… is not sumpthin' ya do when preparin' a steak fer the barbecue grill. It's when you overdo sumpthin'.

TO FAN OUT:

… means to
spread out
and look for
sumpthin'.

TO FIRE AWAY:

… has nuthin' to do with going huntin'
or in time of war. It means to begin sumpthin' or
to continue, as in, "When he's finished talkin',
then you fire away."

TO GET HITCHED:

... is not always what you do to a team of horses. It also refers to when a couple gets married.

TO SKEEDADDLE:

... is to hurry and leave. Or you might cut-out, split, skip out, make tracks, make oneself scarce, vamoose, shove off, light out, high- tail it out of there, take a powder or scram.

TO SOFT-SOAP:

... is to pile on compliments
to someone in order
to reap certain
benefits. And a
blatherskite is
someone who tries
to soft-soap some-
one else or just
plain talks a
lot.

TWO AXE-HANDLES WIDE:

... means broad or very wide, as in, "That fat
gal's backside was 'bout two axe-handles wide!!"

UGLY AS SIN OR AS A MUD FENCE:

... is said about
a very
unattractive
person.

UP THE CREEK WITHOUT A PADDLE:

… means you're in trouble.

UP TO SNUFF:

… means all right, as in, "When Henry made a deposit in his savings account, he checked the total and found everything as up to snuff."

VEGGETIBLES:

... that's what
ya raise in yer garden —
like tomaters, corn on
the cob, head lettuce,
peas, and string
beans.

WARSH:

Back not so many
years ago, women
used ta do the
fambly warshin'
on a "warsh-
board".

WHIP THE TIGER:

To whip the tiger is to git lucky and win at gamblin'.

WHISTLIN' AIN'T WHAT MAKES THE PLOW GO:

This means that you have to bend yer back to git sumpthin' done. Ya can't just sit back and let it do itself.

WHITE LIGHTNIN':

White lightnin' is whiskey that looks like water and kicks like a mule!!

WINDER:

... window, as in, "Why doncha shut the winder? It's a-gittin' mighty chilly in here!"

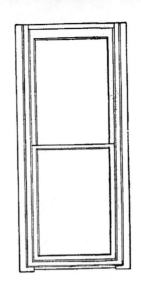

WINDY:

... is not in regard ta the weather. It's when someone is full of "hot air", as in, "That old geezer's as windy as a March day."

WING-DING:

... has nuthin' ta do with a bird. It's a fit of anger, as in, "That kid is so spoiled rotten and lazy that when he don't git his way, he throws a wing-ding."

WISENHEIMER:

... is not the name of a Jewish rabbi. It is a smart aleck or know it all, as in, "He acts like such a wisenheimer when you ask him a question."

WISHY-WASHY:

… means that someone is weak and has no backbone.

WOOIN' OR COURTIN':

… is when two people of the opposite sex are dating.
When they're being amorous or affectionate, they might be lollygaggin', actin' lovey-dovey, neckin', smoochin', pitchin' woo, makin' eyes at each other, or actin' mushy, If they're fallin' in love, it might be called puppy love or calf love, or that they're crazy over each other or goofy about one another, sweet on, stuck on, have a crush on each other, are moon-struck or cow-simple.

WRENCH:

After warshing the clothes, the women — in olden times — "wrenched" them in a galvanized tub or a wooden tub of water.

WUNST:

... once, as in, "If I telled ya wunst, I've telled ya twice, quit sloppin' booze on ma arm."

YAHOOS:

This is an expression used ta describe several kids, greenhorns, or a bunch of people.

YA LOOK LIKE SUMPTHIN' THE CATS DRUG IN:

...applied to a person who looks totally disheveled.

NEED A GIFT?

for

• Shower • Birthday • Mother's Day •
• Anniversary • Christmas •

Turn Page for Order Form
(Order Now While Supply Lasts!)

To Order Copies Of
HOW TO TALK HOOSIER

Please send me _____copies of **How to Talk Hoosier** at $7.95 each. (Make checks payable to **QUIXOTE PRESS**.) Add $2.15 for shipping and handling per book. _____

Total: _____

(Make checks payable to **QUIXOTE PRESS**.)

Name _____

Street _____

City _____ State _____ Zip _____

Send Orders To:
Quixote Press
1854 - 345th Ave.
Wever, IA 52658
1-800-571-2665

- -

To Order Copies Of
HOW TO TALK HOOSIER

Please send me _____copies of **How to Talk Hoosier** at $7.95 each. (Make checks payable to **QUIXOTE PRESS**.) Add $2.15 for shipping and handling per book. _____

Total: _____

(Make checks payable to **QUIXOTE PRESS**.)

Name _____

Street _____

City _____ State _____ Zip _____

Send Orders To:
Quixote Press
1854 - 345th Ave.
Wever, IA 52658
1-800-571-2665

Since you have enjoyed this book, perhaps you would be interested in some of these others from **QUIXOTE PRESS**.

ARKANSAS BOOKS

ARKANSAS' ROADKILL COOKBOOK
        by Bruce Carlson . . . . .paperback $7.95
REVENGE OF ROADKILL
        by Bruce Carlson . . . . .paperback $7.95
LET'S US GO DOWN TO THE RIVER 'N...
        by Various Authors . . . . .paperback $9.95
TALL TALES OF THE MISSISSIPPI RIVER
        by Dan Titus . . . . .paperback $9.95
LOST & BURIED TREASURE OF THE MISSISSIPPI RIVER
        by Netha Bell & Gary Scholl . . . . .paperback $9.95
TALES OF HACKETT'S CREEK
        by Dan Titus . . . . .paperback $9.95
101 WAYS TO USE A DEAD RIVER FLY
        by Bruce Carlson . . . . .paperback $7.95
VACANT LOT, SCHOOL YARD & BACK ALLEY GAMES
        by Various Authors . . . . .paperback $9.95
HOW TO TALK MIDWESTERN
        by Robert Thomas . . . . .paperback $7.95
ARKANSAS COOKIN'
        by Bruce Carlson . . . .(3x5) paperback $5.95

DAKOTA BOOKS

HOW TO TALK DAKOTA . . . . .paperback $7.95
Some Pretty Tame, but Kinda Funny Stories About Early
DAKOTA LADIES-OF-THE-EVENING
        by Bruce Carlson . . . . .paperback $9.95
SOUTH DAKOTA ROADKILL COOKBOOK
        by Bruce Carlson . . . . .paperback $7.95

REVENGE OF ROADKILL

by Bruce Carlson ....paperback $7.95

101 WAYS TO USE A DEAD RIVER FLY

by Bruce Carlson ....paperback $7.95

LET'S US GO DOWN TO THE RIVER 'N...

by Various Authors ....paperback $9.95

LOST & BURIED TREASURE OF THE MISSOURI RIVER

by Netha Bell ....paperback $9.95

MAKIN' DO IN SOUTH DAKOTA

by Various Authors ....paperback $9.95

THE DAKOTAS' VANSHING OUTHOUSE

by Bruce Carlson ....paperback $9.95

VACANT LOT, SCHOOL YARD & BACK ALLEY GAMES

by Various Authors ....paperback $9.95

HOW TO TALK MIDWESTERN

by Robert Thomas ....paperback $7.95

DAKOTA COOKIN'

by Bruce Carlson ....(3x5) paperback $5.95

ILLINOIS BOOKS

ILLINOIS COOKIN'

by Bruce Carlson ....(3x5) paperback $5.95

THE VANISHING OUTHOUSE OF ILLINOIS

by Bruce Carlson ....paperback $9.95

A FIELD GUIDE TO ILLINOIS' CRITTERS

by Bruce Carlson ....paperback $7.95

Some Pretty Tame, but Kinda Funny Stories About Early
ILLINOIS LADIES-OF-THE-EVENING

by Bruce Carlson ....paperback $9.95

ILLINOIS' ROADKILL COOKBOOK
>   by Bruce Carlson ....paperback $7.95
101 WAYS TO USE A DEAD RIVER FLY
>   by Bruce Carlson ....paperback $7.95
HOW TO TALK ILLINOIS
>   by Netha Bell ....paperback $7.95
TALL TALES OF THE MISSISSIPPI RIVER
>   by Dan Titus ....paperback $9.95
TALES OF HACKETT'S CREEK
>   by Dan Titus ....paperback $9.95
LOST & BURIED TREASURE OF THE MISSISSIPPI RIVER
>   by Netha Bell & Gary Scholl ....paperback $9.95
STRANGE FOLKS ALONG THE MISSISSIPPI
>   by Pat Wallace ....paperback $9.95
LET'S US GO DOWN TO THE RIVER 'N...
>   by Various Authors ....paperback $9.95
MISSISSIPPI RIVER PO' FOLK
>   by Pat Wallace ....paperback $9.95
GHOSTS OF THE MISSISSIPPI RIVER
(from Keokuk to St. Louis)
>   by Bruce Carlson ....paperback $9.95
GHOSTS OF THE MISSISSIPPI RIVER
 (from Dubuque to Keokuk)
>   by Bruce Carlson ....paperback $9.95
MAKIN' DO IN ILLINOIS
>   by Various Authors ....paperback $9.95
MY VERY FIRST
>   by Various Authors ....paperback $9.95
VACANT LOT, SCHOOL YARD & BACK ALLEY GAMES
>   by Various Authors ....paperback $9.95
HOW TO TALK MIDWESTERN
>   by Robert Thomas ....paperback $7.95

INDIANA BOOKS

HOW TO TALK HOOSIER
        By Netha Bell .paperback $7.95
REVENGE OF ROADKILL
        by Bruce Carlson . . . . .paperback $7.95
LET'S US GO DOWN TO THE RIVER 'N...
        by Various Authors . . . . .paperback $9.95
101 WAYS TO USE A DEAD RIVER FLY
        by Bruce Carlson . . . . .paperback $7.95
VACANT LOT, SCHOOL YARD & BACK ALLEY GAMES
        by Various Authors . . . . .paperback $9.95
HOW TO TALK MIDWESTERN
        by Robert Thomas . . . . .paperback $7.95
INDIANA PRAIRIE SKIRTS
        by Bev Faaborg & Lois Brinkman . . . . .paperback $9.95
INDIANA COOKIN'
        by Bruce Carlson . . . .(3x5) paperback $5.95

IOWA BOOKS

IOWA COOKIN'
        by Bruce Carlson . . . .(3x5) paperback $5.95
IOWA'S ROADKILL COOKBOOK
        by Bruce Carlson . . . . .paperback $7.95
REVENGE OF ROADKILL
        by Bruce Carlson . . . . .paperback $7.95
GHOSTS OF THE AMANA COLONIES
        by Lori Erickson . . . . .paperback $9.95
GHOSTS OF THE IOWA GREAT LAKES
        by Bruce Carlson . . . . .paperback $9.95
GHOSTS OF THE MISSISSIPPI RIVER
(from Dubuque to Keokuk)
        by Bruce Carlson . . . . .paperback $9.95

GHOSTS OF THE MISSISSIPPI RIVER
(from Minneapolis to Dubuque)
       by Bruce Carlson ....paperback $9.95
GHOSTS OF POLK COUNTY, IOWA
       by Tom Welch ....paperback $9.95
TALES OF HACKETT'S CREEK
       by Dan Titus ....paperback $9.95
TALL TALES OF THE MISSISSIPPI RIVER
       by Dan Titus ....paperback $9.95
101 WAYS TO USE A DEAD RIVER FLY
       by Bruce Carlson ....paperback $7.95
LET'S US GO DOWN TO THE RIVER 'N...
       by Various Authors ....paperback $9.95
TRICKS WE PLAYED IN IOWA
       by Various Authors ....paperback $9.95
IOWA, THE LAND BETWEEN THE VOWELS
(farm boy stories from the early 1900s)
       by Bruce Carlson ....paperback $9.95
LOST & BURIED TREASURE OF THE MISSISSIPPI RIVER
       by Netha Bell & Gary Scholl ....paperback $9.95
Some Pretty Tame, but Kinda Funny Stories About Early
IOWA LADIES-OF-THE-EVENING
       by Bruce Carlson ....paperback $9.95
THE VANISHING OUTHOUSE OF IOWA
       by Bruce Carlson ....paperback $9.95
IOWA'S EARLY HOME REMEDIES
       by 26 Students at Wapello Elem. School ..paperback $9.95
IOWA - A JOURNEY IN A PROMISED LAND
       by Kathy Yoder ....paperback $16.95
LOST & BURIED TREASURE OF THE MISSOURI RIVER
       by Netha Bell ....paperback $9.95
FIELD GUIDE TO IOWA'S CRITTERS
       by Bruce Carlson ....paperback $7.95
OLD IOWA HOUSES, YOUNG LOVES
       by Bruce Carlson ....paperback $9.95

SKUNK RIVER ANTHOLOGY
    by Gene Olson . . . . .paperback $9.95
VACANT LOT, SCHOOL YARD & BACK ALLEY GAMES
    by Various Authors . . . . .paperback $9.95
HOW TO TALK MIDWESTERN
    by Robert Thomas . . . . .paperback $7.95

KANSAS BOOKS

HOW TO TALK KANSAS . . . . .paperback $7.95
STOPOVER IN KANSAS
    by Jon McAlpin .paperback $9.95
LET'S US GO DOWN TO THE RIVER 'N...
    by Various Authors . . . . .paperback $9.95
LOST & BURIED TREASURE OF THE MISSOURI RIVER
    by Netha Bell . . . . .paperback $9.95
101 WAYS TO USE A DEAD RIVER FLY
    by Bruce Carlson . . . . .paperback $7.95
VACANT LOT, SCHOOL YARD & BACK ALLEY GAMES
    by Various Authors . . . . .paperback $9.95
HOW TO TALK MIDWESTERN
    by Robert Thomas . . . . .paperback $7.95

KENTUCKY BOOKS

TALES OF HACKETT'S CREEK
    by Dan Titus . . . . .paperback $9.95
LOST & BURIED TREASURE OF THE MISSISSIPPI RIVER
    by Netha Bell & Gary Scholl . . . . .paperback $9.95
LET'S US GO DOWN TO THE RIVER 'N...
    by Various Authors . . . . .paperback $9.95

101 WAYS TO USE A DEAD RIVER FLY
by Bruce Carlson ....paperback $7.95
TALL TALES OF THE MISSISSIPPI RIVER
by Dan Titus ....paperback $9.95
MY VERY FIRST
by Various Authors ....paperback $9.95
VACANT LOT, SCHOOL YARD & BACK ALLEY GAMES
by Various Authors ....paperback $9.95

MICHIGAN BOOKS

MICHIGAN COOKIN'
by Bruce Carlson ....paperback $7.95
MICHIGAN'S ROADKILL COOKBOOK
by Bruce Carlson ....paperback $7.95
MICHIGAN'S VANISHING OUTHOUSE
by Bruce Carlson ....paperback $9.95

MINNESOTA BOOKS

MINNESOTA'S ROADKILL COOKBOOK
by Bruce Carlson ....paperback $7.95
REVENGE OF ROADKILL
by Bruce Carlson ....paperback $7.95
GHOSTS OF THE MISSISSIPPI RIVER
(from Minneapolis to Dubuque)
by Bruce Carlson ....paperback $9.95
LAKES COUNTRY COOKBOOK
by Bruce Carlson ....paperback $11.95

TALES OF HACKETT'S CREEK
by Dan Titus . . . . .paperback $9.95
MINNESOTA'S VANISHING OUTHOUSE
by Bruce Carlson . . . . .paperback $9.95
TALL TALES OF THE MISSISSIPPI RIVER
by Dan Titus . . . . .paperback $9.95
Some Pretty Tame, but Kinda Funny Stories About Early
MINNESOTA LADIES-OF-THE-EVENING
by Bruce Carlson . . . . .paperback $9.95
101 WAYS TO USE A DEAD RIVER FLY
by Bruce Carlson . . . . .paperback $7.95
LOST & BURIED TEASURE OF THE MISSISSIPPI RIVER
by Netha Bell & Gary Scholl . . . . .paperback $9.95
VACANT LOT, SCHOOL YARD & BACK ALLEY GAMES
by Various Authors . . . . .paperback $9.95
HOW TO TALK MIDWESTERN
by Robert Thomas . . . . .paperback $7.95
MINNESOTA COOKIN'
by Bruce Carlson . . . .(3x5) paperback $5.95

MISSOURI BOOKS

MISSOURI COOKIN'
by Bruce Carlson . . . .(3x5) paperback $5.95
MISSOURI'S ROADKILL COOKBOOK
by Bruce Carlson . . . . .paperback $7.95
REVENGE OF THE ROADKILL
by Bruce Carlson . . . . .paperback $7.95
LET'S US GO DOWN TO THE RIVER 'N...
by Various Authors . . . . .paperback $9.95

LAKES COUNTRY COOKBOOK
by Bruce Carlson . . . . .paperback $11.95

101 WAYS TO USE A DEAD RIVER FLY
by Bruce Carlson . . . . .paperback $7.95

TALL TALES OF THE MISSISSIPPI RIVER
by Dan Titus . . . . .paperback $9.95

TALES OF HACKETT'S CREEK
by Dan Titus . . . . .paperback $9.95

STRANGE FOLKS ALONG THE MISSISSIPPI
by Pat Wallace . . . . .paperback $9.95

LOST AND BURIED TREASURE OF THE MISSOURI RIVER
by Netha Bell .paperback $9.95

HOW TO TALK MISSOURIAN
by Bruce Carlson . . . . .paperback $7.95

VACANT LOT, SCHOOL YARD & BACK ALLEY GAMES
by Various Authors . . . . .paperback $9.95

HOW TO TALK MIDWESTERN
by Robert Thomas . . . . .paperback $7.95

LOST & BURIED TREASURE OF THE MISSISSIPPI RIVER
by Netha Bell & Gary Scholl . . . . .paperback $9.95

MISSISSIPPI RIVER PO' FOLK
by Pat Wallace . . . . .paperback $9.95

Some Pretty Tame, but Kinda Funny Stories About Early
MISSOURI LADIES-OF-THE-EVENING
by Bruce Carlson . . . . .paperback $9.95

A FIELD GUIDE TO MISSOURI'S CRITTERS
by Bruce Carlson . . . . .paperback $7.95

EARLY MISSOURI HOME REMEDIES
by Various Authors . . . . .paperback $9.95

UNDERGROUND MISSOURI
by Bruce Carlson . . . . .paperpback $9.95

MISSISSIPPI RIVER COOKIN' BOOK
by Bruce Carlson . . . . .paperback $11.95

NEBRASKA BOOKS

LOST & BURIED TREASURE OF THE MISSOURI RIVER
     by Netha Bell .paperback $9.95
101 WAYS TO USE A DEAD RIVER FLY
     by Bruce Carlson . . . . .paperback $7.95
LET'S US GO DOWN TO THE RIVER 'N...
     by Various Authors . . . . .paperback $9.95
HOW TO TALK MIDWESTERN
     by Robert Thomas . . . . .paperback $7.95
VACANT LOT, SCHOOL YARD & BACK ALLEY GAMES
     by Various Authors . . . . .paperback $9.95

TENNESSEE BOOKS

TALES OF HACKETT'S CREEK
     by Dan Titus . . . . .paperback $9.95
TALL TALES OF THE MISSISSIPPI RIVER
     by Dan Titus . . . . .paperback $9.95
UNSOLVED MYSTERIES OF THE MISSISSIPPI
     by Netha Bell .paperback $9.95
LOST & BURIED TREASURE OF THE MISSISSIPPI RIVER
     by Netha Bell & Gary Scholl . . . . .paperback $9.95
LET'S US GO DOWN TO THE RIVER 'N...
     by Various Authors . . . . .paperback $9.95
101 WAYS TO USE A DEAD RIVER FLY
     by Bruce Carlson . . . . .paperback $7.95
VACANT LOT, SCHOOL YARD & BACK ALLEY GAMES
     by Various Authors . . . . .paperback $9.95

WISCONSIN

HOW TO TALK WISCONSIN . . . . .paperback $7.95
WISCONSIN COOKIN'
        by Bruce Carlson . . . .(3x5) paperback $5.95
WISCONSIN'S ROADKILL COOKBOOK
        by Bruce Carlson . . . . .paperback $7.95
REVENGE OF ROADKILL
        by Bruce Carlson . . . . .paperback $7.95
TALL TALES OF THE MISSISSIPPI RIVER
        by Dan Titus .paperback $9.95
LAKES COUNTRY COOKBOOK
        by Bruce Carlson . . . . .paperback $11.95
TALES OF HACKETT'S CREEK
        by Dan Titus .paperback $9.95
LET'S US GO DOWN TO THE RIVER 'N...
        by Various Authors . . . . .paperback $9.95
101 WAYS TO USE A DEAD RIVER FLY
        by Bruce Carlson . . . . .paperback $7.95
LOST & BURIED TREASURE OF THE MISSISSIPPI RIVER
        by Netha Bell & Gary Scholl . . . . .paperback $9.95
HOW TO TALK MIDWESTERN
        by Robert Thomas . . . . .paperback $7.95
VACANT LOT, SCHOOL YARD & BACK ALLEY GAMES
        by Various Authors . . . . .paperback $9.95
MY VERY FIRST
        by Various Authors . . . . .paperback $9.95
EARLY WISCONSIN HOME REMEDIES
        by Various Authors . . . . .paperback $9.95
THE VANISHING OUTHOUSE OF WISCONSIN
        by Bruce Carlson . . . . .paperback $9.95
GHOSTS OF DOOR COUNTY, WISCONSIN
        by Geri Rider .paperback $9.95

RIVER BOOKS

ON THE SHOULDERS OF A GIANT
    by M. Cody and D. Walker . . . . .paperback $9.95
SKUNK RIVER ANTHOLOGY
    by Gene "Will" Olson . . . . .paperback $9.95
JACK KING vs DETECTIVE MACKENZIE
    by Netha Bell .paperback $9.95
LOST & BURIED TREASURE OF THE MISSISSIPPI RIVER
    by Netha Bell & Gary Scholl . . . . .paperback $9.95
MISSISSIPPI RIVER PO' FOLK
    by Pat Wallace . . . . .paperback $9.95
STRANGE FOLKS ALONG THE MISSISSIPPI
    by Pat Wallace . . . . .paperback $9.95
TALES OF HACKETT'S CREEK
(1940s Mississippi River kids)
    by Dan Titus . . . . .paperback $9.95
101 WAYS TO USE A DEAD RIVER FLY
    by Bruce Carlson . . . . .paperback $7.95
LET'S US GO DOWN TO THE RIVER 'N...
    by Various Authors . . . . .paperback $9.95
LOST & BURIED TREASURE OF THE MISSOURI
    by Netha Bell .paperback $9.95
LIL' RED BOOK OF FISHING TIPS
    by Tom Hollatz . . . . .paperback $7.95

COOKBOOKS

THE BACK-TO-THE SUPPER TABLE COOKBOOK
    by Susie Babbington . . . . .paperback $11.95
THE COVERED BRIDGES COOKBOOK
    by Bruce Carlson . . . . .paperback $11.95
COUNTRY COOKING-RECIPES OF MY AMISH HERITAGE
    by Kathy Yoder . . . . .paperback $9.95
CIVIL WAR COOKIN', STORIES, 'N SUCH
    by Darlene Funkhouser . . . . .paperback $9.95

SOUTHERN HOMEMADE
  by Lorraine Lott . . . . .paperback $11.95
THE ORCHARD, BERRY PATCHES, AND GARDEN CKBK
  by Bruce Carlson . . . . .paperback $11.95
THE BODY SHOP COOKBOOK
  by Sherrill Wolff . . . . .paperback $14.95
CAMP COOKING COOKBOOK
  by Mary Ann Kerl . . . . .paperback $9.95
FARMERS' MARKET COOKBOOK
  by Bruce Carlson . . . . .paperback $9.95
HERBAL COOKERY
  by Dixie Stephen . . . . .paperback $9.95
MAD ABOUT GARLIC
  by Pat Reppert . . . . .paperback $9.95
BREADS! BREADS! BREADS!
  by Mary Ann Kerl . . . . .paperback $9.95
PUMPKIN PATCHES, PROVERBS & PIES
  by Cherie Reilly . . . . .paperback $9.95
ARIZONA COOKING
  by Barbara Soden . . . . .paperback $5.95
SOUTHWEST COOKING
  by Barbara Soden . . . . .paperback $5.95
EATIN' OHIO
  by Rus Pishnery . . . . .paperback $9.95
EATIN' ILLINOIS
  by Rus Pishnery . . . . .paperback $9.95
KENTUCKY COOKIN'
  by Marilyn Tucker Carlson . . . . .paperback $5.95
INDIANA COOKIN'
  by Bruce Carlson . . . . .paperback $5.95
KANSAS COOKIN'
  by Bruce Carlson . . . . .paperback $5.95

NEW JERSEY COOKING
by Bruce Carlson ....paperback $5.95
NEW MEXICO COOKING
by Barbara Soden ....paperback $5.95
NEW YORK COOKIN'
by Bruce Carlson ....paperback $5.95
OHIO COOKIN'
by Bruce Carlson ....paperback $5.95
PENNSYLVANIA COOKING
by Bruce Carlson ....paperback $5.95
AMISH-MENNONITE STRAWBERRY COOKBOOK
by Alta Kauffman ....paperback $5.95
APPLES! APPLES! APPLES!
by Melissa Mosley ....paperback $5.95
APPLES GALORE!!!
by Bruce Carlson ....paperback $5.95
BERRIES! BERRIES! BERRIES!
by Melissa Mosley ....paperback $5.95
BERRIES GALORE!!!
by Bruce Carlson ....paperback $5.95
CHERRIES! CHERRIES! CHERRIES!
by Marilyn Carlson ....paperback $5.95
CITRUS! CITRUS! CITRUS!
by Lisa Nafziger ....paperback $5.95
COOKING WITH CIDER
by Bruce Carlson ....paperback $5.95
COOKING WITH THINGS THAT GO BAA
by Bruce Carlson ....paperback $5.95
COOKING WITH THINGS THAT GO CLUCK
by Bruce Carlson ....paperback $5.95
COOKING WITH THINGS THAT GO MOO
by Bruce Carlson ....paperback $5.95
COOKING WITH THINGS THAT GO OINK
by Bruce Carlson ....paperback $5.95

GARLIC! GARLIC! GARLIC!
> by Bruce Carlson .... paperback $5.95

KID COOKIN'
> by Bev Faaborg .... paperback $5.95

THE KID'S GARDEN FUN BOOK
> by Theresa McKeown .... paperback $5.95

KID'S PUMPKIN FUN BOOK
> by J. Ballhagen .... paperback $5.95

NUTS! NUTS! NUTS!
> by Melissa Mosley .... paperback $5.95

PEACHES! PEACHES! PEACHES!
> by Melissa Mosley .... paperback $5.95

PUMPKINS! PUMPKINS! PUMPKINS!
> by Melissa Mosley .... paperback $5.95

VEGGIE-FRUIT-NUT MUFFIN RECIPES
> by Darlene Funkhouser .... paperback $5.95

WORKING GIRL COOKING
> by Bruce Carlson .... paperback $5.95

SOME LIKE IT HOT!!!
> by Barbara Soden .... paperback $5.95

HOW TO COOK SALSA
> by Barbara Soden .... paperback $5.95

COOKING WITH FRESH HERBS
> by Eleanor Wagner .... paperback $5.95

BUFFALO COOKING
> by Momfeather .... paperback $5.95

NO STOVE-NO SHARP KNIFE KIDS NO-COOK COOKBOOK
> by Timmy Denning .... paperback $9.95

HALLOWEEN
    by Bruce Carlson . . . . .paperback $9.95
VEGGIE TALK
    by Glynn Singleton . . . . .paperback $6.95
WASHASHORE
    by Margaret Potter . . . . .paperback $9.95
PRINCES AND TOADS
    by Dr. Sharon Tobler . . . . .paperback $12.95
HOW SOON CAN YOU GET HERE, DOC?
    by David Wynia, DVM . . . . .paperback $9.95
MY PAW WAS A GREAT DANE
    by R. E. Rasmussen, DVM . . . . .paperback $14.95

To order any of these books from Quixote Press call 1-800-571-2665